The Life of a
GRASSHOPPER

Clare Hibbert

www.raintreepublishers.co.uk

Visit our website to find out more information about **Raintree** books.

To order:
- ☎ Phone 44 (0) 1865 888112
- 🖹 Send a fax to 44 (0) 1865 314091
- 🖳 Visit the Raintree Bookshop at **www.raintreepublishers.co.uk** to browse our catalogue and order online.

First published in Great Britain by Raintree, Halley Court, Jordan Hill, Oxford OX2 8EJ, part of Harcourt Education.
Raintree is a registered trademark of Harcourt Education Ltd.

Editorial: Nick Hunter and Catherine Clarke
Design: Michelle Lisseter and Tipani Design
(www.tipani.co.uk)
Illustration: Tony Jones, Art Construction
Picture Research: Maria Joannou and Elaine Willis
Production: Jonathan Smith

Originated by Dot Gradations Ltd
Printed and bound in China by South China Printing Company

ISBN 1 844 43303 X
08 07 06 05 04
10 9 8 7 6 5 4 3 2 1

British Library Cataloguing in Publication Data
Hibbert, Clare
The Life of a Grasshopper. – (Life Cycles)
571.8'15726
A full catalogue record for this book is available from the British Library.

Acknowledgements
The publishers would like to thank the following for permission to reproduce photographs:
Ardea (Bob Gibbons) p. **13**, Corbis pp. **9**, **26** (Chris Hellier); Ecoscene p. **20**; FLPA pp. **4** (S. & D. & K. Maslowski), **5** (Robin Chittenden), **11** (A. R. Hamblin), **14** (B Borrell Casals), **15** (Simon Hosking), **17** (Robin Chittenden), **19** (D. Malowski), **21** (A. Calegari/Panda), **23**, **24** (Ron Austing), **25** (Larry West), **27** (J. C. Allen), **28** (Mark Newman), **29** (Larry West); Getty Images (Imagebank) p. **18**; NHPA pp. **16** (Stephen Dalton), **22** (Eric Soder); Oxford Scientific Films pp. **8**, **10**; Premaphotos Wildlife (Ken Preston-Mafham) p. **12**.

Cover photograph of a grasshopper, reproduced with permission of Premaphotos Wildlife.

The publishers would like to thank Janet Stott for her assistance in the preparation of this book.

Every effort has been made to contact copyright holders of any material reproduced in this book. Any omissions will be rectified in subsequent printings if notice is given to the publishers.

The paper used to print this book comes from sustainable resources.

Contents

Any words appearing in bold, **like this**, are explained in the Glossary.

The grasshopper

Grasshoppers belong to a family of animals called **insects**. Other insects include bees and ladybirds. Like all insects, a grasshopper has three parts to its body and three pairs of legs. The back legs are strong and powerful. The grasshopper uses them for jumping. Adult grasshoppers also have two pairs of wings for flying.

head

feeler

thorax

The three main parts of an insect's body are its head, thorax and abdomen.

leg

abdomen

Growing up

Just as you grow bigger year by year, grasshoppers grow and change too. Different types of grasshopper grow at different speeds, but they all go through the same changes. The different stages of the grasshopper's life make up its **life cycle**.

This adult grasshopper is resting on a stick.

Where grasshoppers live

Grasshoppers are found in almost every part of the world, especially in warm places. The place where an animal lives is called its **habitat**. Fields and grasslands are good habitats for grasshoppers. There is plenty of food to eat and places to hide.

A grasshopper's life

The grasshopper's **life cycle** begins in late summer when a female grasshopper lays her eggs. Inside each egg, a baby grasshopper develops. While it is inside the egg, the grasshopper is called an **embryo**. When spring comes, the egg **hatches**. A young grasshopper, called a **nymph**, comes out of it. It looks a bit like an adult, but it is smaller and does not have wings.

From nymph to adult

Over the next month or so, the grasshopper nymph sheds its skin about five times. Each time, the nymph's body looks more like an adult's. Finally, the **insect** is an adult. It can fly, and it can **reproduce** – that is, make its own baby grasshoppers. A grasshopper's life as an adult lasts only a month or two.

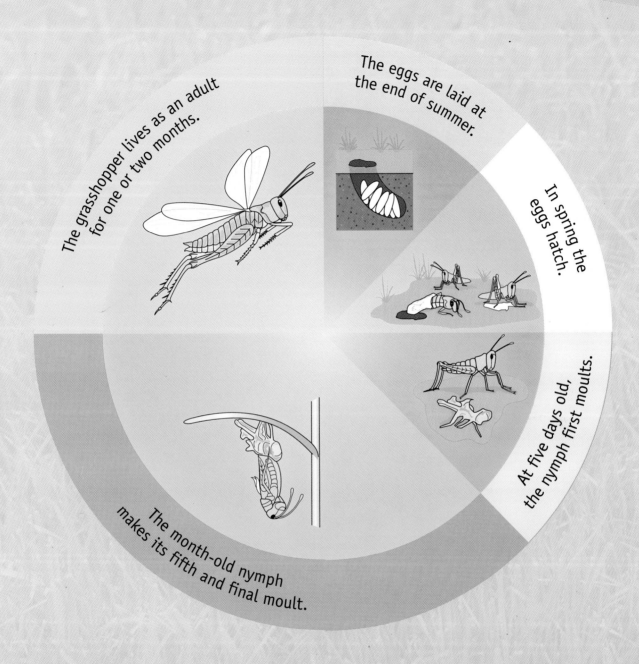

The eggs are laid at the end of summer.

In spring the eggs hatch.

At five days old, the nymph first moults.

The month-old nymph makes its fifth and final moult.

The grasshopper lives as an adult for one or two months.

This diagram shows the life cycle of a grasshopper, from egg to adult.

Hidden eggs

Grasshopper eggs are laid at the end of summer. The female grasshopper sticks the end of her body into the soil and pushes out some eggs. She might lay as few as 6 eggs, or as many as 150. They are stuck together in a kind of foam. The foam hardens into a sausage-shape, called a **pod**.

Once the egg pod has hardened, it is waterproof. The pod acts as a raincoat for the eggs inside.

Egg action

Each egg is about half a centimetre long – smaller than a pea. At first, the inside is mostly **yolk**. This is food for the growing **embryo**. The embryo grows until it fills almost the whole egg. Then, the ground outside the pod gets very cold. It is winter. The embryo stops growing. It is dormant – in a sort of sleep – until the spring.

A grasshopper could not cope with the winter cold. The eggs hatch in spring, when all the snow has melted.

Pod snack

Not all the eggs make it through winter. Some pods are eaten away from the inside, by tiny wasps and flies whose parents burrowed into the soil and laid their eggs inside the grasshopper's eggs. Others are munched by beetle **grubs** in the soil, or dug up by hungry field mice and frogs.

Hatching

In spring, the snows thaw and the soil warms up. The warmth wakes up the **embryo**. It finishes growing. Now it has been inside the egg for ten months. It fills the whole egg and is ready to **hatch**. All the eggs in the **pod** hatch in the same few minutes.

These nymphs are hatching out of their eggs.

On the move

The grasshopper youngsters are called **nymphs.** Each one is wrapped in a kind of skin. It wriggles up through the soil, then rolls around on the ground to shake off the skin. The nymph's body is soft, but it soon dries hard in the sun. Now the nymph jumps away – quick! – before ants and other hunters find it.

These wood ants are dragging a dead grasshopper back to their nest.

Ant attack

Ants are **insects** that live together in groups. They are **predators**, which means that they hunt and eat other animals for food. Working together, the ants attack and eat grasshopper nymphs. They bite with their sharp jaws.

Mini hopper

By the time the **nymph** is about five days old, its skin is too tight – just like clothes that you have grown out of. This is no problem for the nymph. The tight skin simply splits and peels off. It looks like a papery grasshopper ghost.

Underneath, the nymph has a brand new skin. This one has more room in it for the growing nymph.

This grasshopper nymph is between moults.

Moulting

On its journey from nymph to adult, the grasshopper will shed its outer skin about five times. This is called moulting. Moulting happens every five days or so.

Changing insects

Young grasshoppers look a lot like their parents. To turn into adult grasshoppers, they only have to change a little. It's not the same for all **insect** young. Caterpillars look nothing like their adult form, butterflies. They have to change their bodies completely.

The nymphs look very like their parents, but they are smaller and do not have wings.

Growing up

Like you, the **nymph** needs food to grow up big and strong. It starts eating right after it is born and carries on eating more and more as it grows. Most grasshoppers eat only plants, but some snack on crunchy **insects**, too.

Can you guess from its name what a grasshopper likes eating best of all? Its favourite foods are grasses. They include farmers' crops, such as wheat, barley, corn, rye and oats.

The nymph has powerful jaws for biting through grasses and leaves.

Top teeth

The leaves of grass plants are tough and stringy. It is amazing that a grasshopper can munch through them – but it has just the jaws for the job.

Grasshoppers have strong mouthparts that can bite down hard enough to chew the leaves.

Sweetcorn

Grasshoppers love maize, the plant that corn-on-the-cob comes from. They eat the stems, leaves and corn kernels. Maize is a living thing with its own **life cycle**. The sweetcorn ripens in the summer sun.

Hop to eat

For the first four weeks of life, the grasshopper **nymph** cannot fly, but it can move quickly. It jumps from plant to plant in search of food. With its long, strong back legs, the grasshopper can leap twenty times its own body length. If you could jump as well as a grasshopper, you would be able to leap over seven cars parked end to end!

Blast off! The grasshopper's powerful legs launch it into the air!

Long legs

Most of the time, the grasshopper's back legs are folded. To jump, it straightens them out and pushes down at the same time. This action catapults it through the air. When they are straightened out, the back legs measure 4 centimetres – which is twice as long as the grasshopper's other legs.

Muscle power

Muscles are stretchy tissues attached to the bones inside every animal's body, including yours. They pull on bones so that we can move. Grasshoppers have very strong muscles in their thighs that make their legs work. The muscles work best when they are warm. That is why grasshoppers like to bask in the sun.

This grasshopper nymph is sunbathing to warm up its muscles.

Danger all around

By the time it is one month old, the **nymph** is nearly an adult. The plumper it grows, the more of a juicy meal it makes. Snakes, toads and birds are all **predators** that like to eat young grasshoppers. There are **insect** predators, too, including the sneaky praying mantis.

This poor nymph has ended up in a roller bird's beak.

Spitting mad

The nymph usually jumps to escape. Sometimes, though, it stays put – and spits! No one really knows why it does this. Perhaps it is trying to confuse the predator.

A praying mantis prepares to attack this grasshopper.

Blending in

The nymph is hard to spot because it is green like the grass. This is called **camouflage**. Some of the predators that eat grasshoppers use the same trick. The grass snake and the praying mantis are both green, too.

Up, up and away

When the **nymph** is about 30 days old, it wriggles out of an old tight skin for the last time. Underneath is its adult body, with wings that allow it to fly. The adult grasshopper has two sets of wings. The outer pair are tough, like leather. They protect the delicate flight wings underneath.

This grasshopper is just finishing its final moult. It is now an adult, with wings!

First flight

The grasshopper launches itself with a jump. As it zooms through the air, its wings start to beat very fast. Soon, it is flying for the first time.

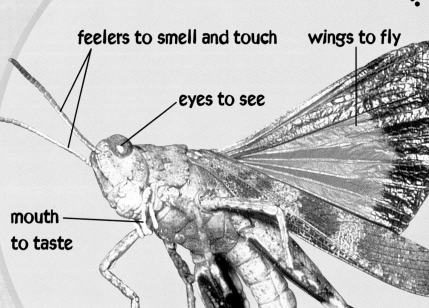

This grasshopper has ...

feelers to smell and touch

wings to fly

eyes to see

mouth to taste

ears on its knees!

Senses

You know about the world by seeing, hearing, touching, smelling and tasting. These are your senses. The grasshopper has senses, too. It has **feelers** to smell and touch. Its mouth tastes. It sees with its eyes but, unlike you, it has five of them. Finally, the grasshopper has ears, but not where you'd expect – many types have ears on their knees!

Finding a mate

Now it is summer. For the first few days of being an adult, a female grasshopper is not ready to **mate**. The **egg placer** at the end of her body is still growing. Once it has finished developing, she is ready to mate.

This male grasshopper is singing to attract a mate.

Sweet sounds

Finding a male is not hard, because males make a chirping noise. You might have heard one when you have been out walking in a park or a field. All the female grasshopper needs to do is follow her ears!

Some male grasshoppers rub their front wings together to produce their song. Others scrape their back leg against one wing, like a violinist uses a bow.

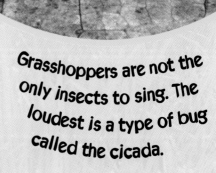

Grasshoppers are not the only insects to sing. The loudest is a type of bug called the cicada.

All kinds of songs

A male grasshopper can sing three different songs. The first is to attract females. When a female is interested, he chirps another song, to encourage her to mate with him. He also has a song for other males, telling them to stay away.

Future nymphs

When they have found each other, the male and female grasshopper **mate**. The male **fertilizes** the female's eggs. Now the eggs will be able to develop into **embryos** and, eventually, **hatch** into **nymphs**.

The female pushes her **egg placer** down into the ground and lays her eggs.

Laying eggs

The female only needs to mate once in her life. After this, all the hundreds of eggs in her body are fertile. She spends the rest of her life – a month or two – finding good places to lay the eggs. She lays groups of eggs in different places and then leaves them. As well as hiding the **pods** in the ground, she lays some in the stems of grasses. Many of the egg pods will be eaten by **predators**, but hopefully some will survive the winter.

Grasshoppers can lay their eggs in sand as well as soil.

Hard times

Most grasshopper adults spend their short lives alone, apart from the time they **mate**. That can all change, however, when there is not much food about. Then, grasshoppers may band together in enormous swarms.

A swarm of locusts. Locusts are a type of grasshopper.

Plague of locusts

The type of grasshopper that is best known for swarming is the locust. One of the biggest-ever swarms was in the USA in 1988. Around 150 billion locusts came together and ate everything in sight. The area they covered was as big as 250,000 soccer pitches. Farmers' crops were ruined.

Killer sprays

Farmers do not like grasshoppers because they eat their crops. Some farmers spray their crops with special, **insect**-killing chemicals. The sprays are called insecticides. Some farmers try to get rid of the grasshoppers another way, by putting animals that eat grasshoppers, such as chickens or ducks, in their fields.

Summer's end

Usually, a grasshopper's adult life lasts only a couple of months during the summer. Many grasshoppers are caught and eaten by **predators**. Those that last the summer start to die off when autumn arrives. The grasshopper's **muscles** won't work in the cold weather and there are not enough green shoots to eat.

In autumn, the grass starts to die back. There is not so much food for a grasshopper to eat.

Final feast

When the grasshopper dies other **insects**, such as robber flies and beetles, move in to feast on its body. All the food and energy that went into building the grasshopper's body does not go to waste.

Already, under the soil, grasshopper **embryos** are starting to grow, ready to begin the **life cycle** all over again.

A robber fly's favourite foods are small wasps and bees, but it will also gobble up the body of a dead grasshopper.

Find out for yourself

The best way to find out more about grasshoppers is to watch them in the wild – look and listen for them in fields. Or you might also see grasshoppers in the zoo, in the insect house.

Books to read

Animal Young: Insects, Rod Theodorou (Heinemann Library, 1999)
I Wonder Why Spiders Spin Webs and Other Questions About Creepy-Crawlies, Amanda O'Neill (Kingfisher Books, 2002)

Using the Internet

Explore the Internet to find out more about grasshoppers. Websites can change, and if some of the links below no longer work, don't worry. Use a search engine, such as www.yahooligans.com, and type in keywords such as 'grasshopper', 'locust' and **'life cycle'**.

Websites

http://www.kidcyber.com.au/topics/grasshops.htm
Find facts about grasshoppers and some great photos too.
http://www.enchantedlearning.com/subjects/insects/orthoptera/grasshopperprintout.shtml
More facts about grasshoppers, plus a picture to print out, label and colour in.

Glossary

camouflage colouring or marks on an animal that allow it to hide from predators

egg placer pointy end of a female insect's body, which is used to lay eggs

embryo baby animal before it has hatched from an egg or been born

feelers also called antennae. Long horns that stick out from an insect's head and are used to sense the world around it.

fertilize join together male and female parts to create the beginnings of a new living thing

grub young insect that looks nothing like its parent. Adult insects have six legs, whereas grubs usually have none.

habitat place where an animal lives

hatch when a young animal comes out of its egg

insect animal that, as an adult, has three parts to its body, three pairs of legs and, usually, two pairs of wings. Grasshoppers, beetles and butterflies are all insects.

life cycle all the different stages in the life of a living thing, such as an animal or plant

mate (verb) when a male and female animal come together to make eggs or babies

muscle stretchy tissue inside the body that allows an animal to move

nymph young insect that is similar to its parent, but will change to reach its adult form

pod casing that contains a grasshopper's eggs

predator animal that hunts other animals and eats them for food

reproduce make babies, eggs or seeds. Adult animals and plants are able to reproduce.

yolk part of an egg that contains food for the growing embryo

Index

Titles in the *Life Cycles* series include:

Hardback   1 844 43300 5

Hardback   1 844 43301 3

Hardback   1 844 43302 1

Hardback   1 844 43303 X

Hardback   1 844 43304 8

Hardback   1 844 43305 6

Find out about the other titles in this series on our website www.raintreepublishers.co.uk